# Ridiculous Relatives

**Paul Cookson** spends most of his time travelling round the country visiting schools, performing his poetry and helping pupils and staff to write their own poems. He has no ridiculous relatives of his own, although his brother is a travelling bonsai tree salesman (he drives a very small van). Paul lives in Retford with his wife and his son – who thinks he's Batman, Superman and Spiderman all rolled into one.

**David Parkins** has illustrated numerous books, ranging from maths textbooks to *The Beano*. His picture books have been shortlisted for the Smarties Book Prize and the Kurt Maschler Award; and commended twice in the National Art Library Illustration Awards. He lives in Lincoln with his wife, three children and six cats.

# Ridiculous Relatives

poems chosen by
**Paul Cookson**

illustrated by
**David Parkins**

MACMILLAN CHILDREN'S BOOKS

Dedicated to the English Department and pupils
at Shelley High School.

First published 1999
by Macmillan Children's Books
a division of Macmillan Publishers Ltd
25 Eccleston Place, London SW1W 9NF
Basingstoke and Oxford

Associated companies throughout the world

ISBN 0 330 37105 3

1 3 5 7 9 8 6 4 2

A CIP catalogue record for this book is available from the British Library.

Printed by Mackays of Chatham plc, Chatham, Kent.

'Cousin Nell' by Roger McGough was first published in *Sporting Relations* by Penguin Books.
'My Electrifying Cousin' (originally entitled 'Electric Fred') and 'Aunty Joan' by John Foster were
first published in *Four O'Clock Friday* by Oxford University Press.

# Contents

# Aunts Across the Sea

My Auntie Quator's very hot,
But poor Aunt Arctica is not.

Aunt Eager's in the Leeward Isles,
Aunt Trim, near Belfast, rarely smiles.

In Belgium lives my dear Aunt Twerp,
Aunt Acid helps to make her burp.

Auntie Clockwise, sad to say,
Always goes round the wrong way.

Auntie Social wears a frown,
Auntie Climax lets you down.

Don't fret if you have bugs or worms –
Auntie Body fights all germs.

Aunts have a lot to Aunts-wer for!
Can you think of any more?

Pam Gidney

# An Interesting Fact About One of my Relatives

My

    great great great great
    great great great great
    great great great great
    great great great great
    great great great great
    great great great great
    great great great great

grandad is very old.

Ian McMillan

# Great-Gran is Manic on her Motorbike

Shout out loud, say what you like
Great-Gran is manic on her motorbike.

Last week her helmet touched the stars
when she zoomed over thirty cars
she didn't quibble, didn't fuss
when they added a double-decker bus.

Shout out loud, say what you like
Great-Gran is manic on her motorbike.

She's a headline hunting, bike stunting
wacky-wild-one-woman-show
she revs and roars to wild applause
there is no place her bike won't go
she gives them shivers jumping rivers
and balancing across high wires
with a cheer she changes gear
flies her bike through blazing tyres.

Shout out loud, say what you like
Great-Gran is manic on her motorbike.

She told me when she quits bike-riding
she's going to take up paragliding
I'll always be her greatest fan
my dazzling, daredevil, manic Great-Gran!

David Harmer

# Mother is a Skinhead

Mother is a skinhead
Brother's heavy metal
Sister's into flower power
So we call her Petal.

Her boyfriend Shane likes techno
He's always on the rave
Grandma is a rapper Yo!
She repeats everything she says
She repeats everything she says.

Dad dresses like Elvis
And greases back his hair.
Grandad likes the seventies
With platform boots and flares.

Uncle Frank's from Worksop
Old punk and tattered clothes
Chains and rings and padlocks
Join his ears to his nose.

Great-Gran dances go go
She likes to shake her thing.
The parrot's into jungle
The budgie's into swing.

Heavy rock at ninety-four years old
Affected Uncle Fred
His bathchair now does ninety-five
And he's got tattoos on his bald head.

Great-Aunt Clara's purple rinse
Shines out like a beacon
Now it's been replaced
With a pink and green Mohican.

Auntie Rene, once removed,
From Italy likes opera.
Uncle Clive likes to jive
But always lands on top of her.

Cousin Ray likes reggae
The baby sings the blues
The dog and cat like rock and roll
Both wear blue suede shoes.

Me . . . I don't like music
Can't sing or play guitar
So I've got the perfect qualities
To be a top pop star.

Rock around the clock, morning, noon and night
No one ever argues, no one ever fights
In tune with each other, a happy family
We'd like to teach the world to sing and live in
    harmony.

Paul Cookson

# Busy Brothers,
# Talented Twins

My twin brother Adam
has just got a job in the circus.

Not on the trapeze or tightrope
he doesn't like heights.

Not as a spangled bareback rider
horses make him sneeze.

Not as a fire-eating juggler
Dad says he mustn't play with matches.

He's become the star attraction
*Adam the Mighty Atom, the World's Youngest Strongman!*

Last week he balanced Mum on his head
lifted Grandad up in his armchair.

Suspended Dad from his teeth by the braces
Gran swung by her bloomers from his big toe.

They were quite impressed
'Coo,' they said, 'this is unusual for a six-year-
old.'

We saw him in the ring last night
in a plastic leopard-skin vest and his PE shorts.

He twirled an elephant on one finger
pushed a car-full of clowns away from his foot.

Ripped up a telephone directory
bent six iron bars and never once dropped his
    teddy.

He asked me to see tomorrow's show
'I'm sorry,' I said, 'I'm leaving for Mars at
teatime.'

'Life's very busy,' I explained,
'when you're the World's Youngest Astronaut.'

David Harmer

# Dad, the Amateur Hypnotist

| | |
|---|---|
| Follow | my |
| swinging | watch |
| with | your |
| eyes. | Now |
| you | are |
| feeling | sleepy . . . |
| When | I |
| count | to |
| three | and |
| click | my |
| fingers, | you |
| will | wake |
| up. | Then |
| you'll | be |
| a | dog. |
| One. | Two. |
| Three. | |

Click!
'Miaow.'

Mike Johnson

# Optical Confusion

A Cyclops and his brother
Keep fighting with each other.
Here's the reason why:
They don't see eye to eye!

Mike Jubb

# Auntie Joan

When Auntie Joan became a phone,
She sat there not saying a thing.
The doctor said, shaking his head,
'You'll just have to give her a ring.'

We had a try, but got no reply.
The tone was always engaged.
'She's just being silly,' said Uncle Billy,
Slamming down the receiver enraged.

'Alas, I fear,' said the engineer,
Who was called in to inspect her,
'I've got no choice. She's lost her voice.
I shall have to disconnect her.'

The phone gave a ring. 'You'll do no such thing,'
Said Auntie's voice on the line.
'I like being a phone. Just leave me alone.
Or else I'll dial nine-nine-nine!'

John Foster

# Arthur Pendragon's Son

When I grow up I'm going to be
an accountant. I've had enough
of swords and dragons,
Celtic Twilights, and quests.
I'm going to live in a semi,
our castle is blooming cold,
I'll have Coke and takeaway pizza,
I hate mead and roasted swan.

When I grow up I'm going to be
an accountant, I've had enough
of Dad at Parents' Evenings
showing me up, in his robe
and sandals, Excalibur at his side,
arguing with my History teacher,
saying all the books are bosh.

When I grow up I'm going to be
an accountant, whether he likes it
or not. I'll have the biggest
colour telly, CD player, video, the lot,
I'll stay home and watch 'Eastenders'
instead of rescuing *damosels,*
listen to the latest Chart Toppers,
and never miss being a prince.

Christine Potter

# Aunt Bertha's Magic Bag

My Aunt Bertha's got a magic bag
Full of lots of wonderful things,
Such as a set of musical spanners
And a mechanical bird that sings.

AND THAT'S NOT ALL . . .

There's also a rat called Erasmus
Who knows how to count to ten,
And a hen which can ride a unicycle
There and back again.

AND THAT'S NOT ALL . . .

She's got an everlasting pink blancmange
Which she eats from time to time,
And a mouse who lives on Edam cheese
And drinks only dandelion wine.

AND THAT'S NOT ALL . . .

There's a pack of cards to tell your fortune
And a four-leaf clover for luck,
Along with a monkey's pogo-stick
And some keys for a ten-ton truck.

# AND THAT'S NOT ALL . . .

There's a treasure map she says
She bought from a famous pirate king,
And a butterfly which flies in circles
Around a golden ring.

AND THAT'S NOT ALL . . .

There's a plastic wind-up hedgehog
That can tap-dance like Fred Astaire
And a letter sent in secret code
From a Transylvanian bear.

AND THAT'S NOT ALL . . .

There's a parrot that can speak Swahili
And whistle any song,
And a woolly wombat who likes to bash
An ancient Chinese gong.

AND THAT'S NOT ALL . . .

There's a ball of string that's ten miles long
And a packet of penguin seed,
And a ticket to the planet Mars
Should you ever feel the need.

There are things you've never seen before,
Things both large and small;
It would need a giant computer
To try and list them all –
At least that's what Aunt Bertha says
She's got inside her bag,
But when I ask if she'll show me them,
She'll just turn to me and say,
'I will, I promise that I will –
One day, one day, one day . . .'

(My Aunt Bertha's like that.)

Tony Langham

# Arthur My Half-Cousin

One eye, one ear, one nostril
One arm, one leg, one hand
Arthur my half-cousin
Is half the boy I am.

One knee, one foot, one ankle
I'm twelve, he's half a dozen
I'm twice the boy that Arthur is
Arthur – half a cousin.

Paul Cookson

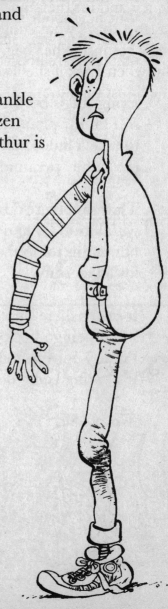

# Little Mummy's Moan

My mum and dad are mummies.
Our neighbour is a sphinx.
We're lying here like dummies,
taking 40 million winks.

Lying still is boring
so I lift my painted lid
to take a little shuffle round
our family pyramid.

They said there'd be an afterlife
with lots to do and see,
but in this tomb there's only gloom
for all eternity.

It seems there's nothing happening
so I'd best go back to bed.
I'm fed up with these bandages.
It's boring being dead.

Tony Mitton

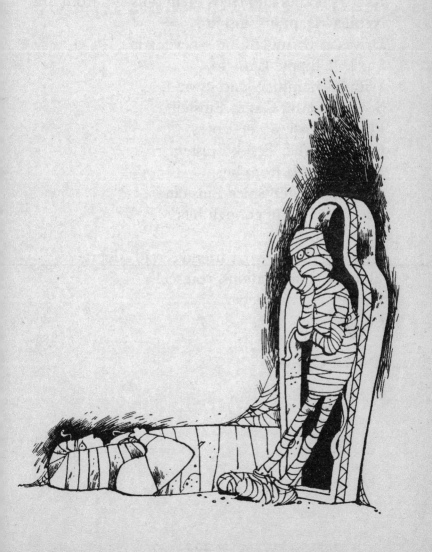

# Albert Einstein's Awful Relatives

There's Great-Aunt Lavinia Einstein,
Keeps poodles and feeds them sausages from tins,
Nephew Damon Einstein,
Drives in Formula One – never wins,
Uncle 'Chippy' Einstein,
With his hammers and saws,
Second cousin Gazza Einstein,
Plays football, never scores,
Clever brother Frank Einstein,
Makes people from bits,
Granddaughter Spice Einstein,
pop singer – not enough hits.

'You can choose your friends,' said Albert,
'But not your relations, you see!'
He called it his theory
Of relativity.

David Orme

# My Electrifying Cousin

Electric Fred has wires in his head
And one hundred watt light bulbs for eyes,
Which means, of course, he can talk in morse
Or flash red, white and blue with surprise.

Just for a lark, he can shoot a spark
For three hundred feet out of his nose.
Wear rubber bands if you shake his hands
Or the current will tingle your toes.

Sometimes he chews a fifteen amp fuse,
Or recharges himself via the fire.
Just give him jolts of thousands of volts
And you'll find he's a really live wire!

John Foster

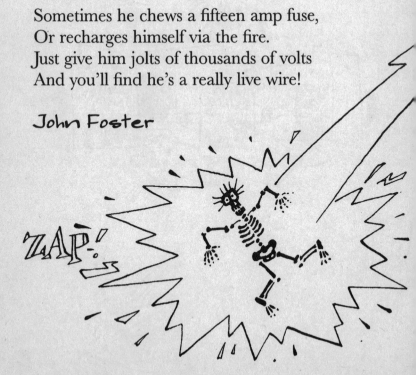

# Legs of my Uncles

Uncle John's are short,
Uncle Stan's are hairy,
Uncle Jim's are long,
Uncle Frank's are scary.

Ian McMillan
Andrew McMillan

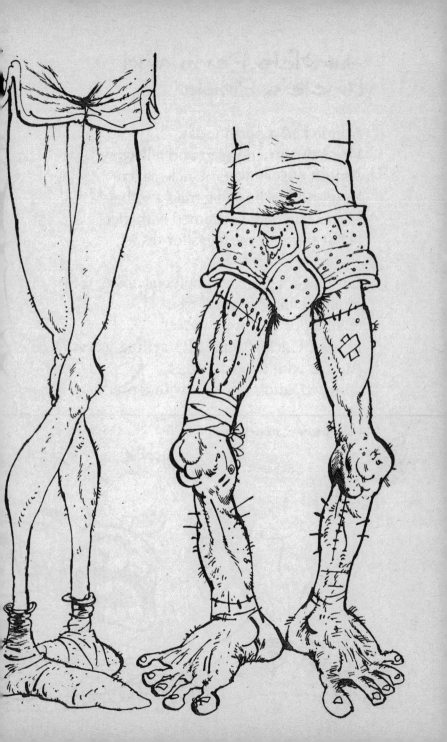

# Auntie's Perm and Uncle's Pimple

Auntie had a perm today.
Her hair turned green and fell away.
At four o'clock when Uncle called
he found her hopping mad and bald.
Uncle quipped, consumed with glee,
'That reminds me, eggs for tea.'

On Uncle's large and bulbous nose,
a pimple like Vesuvius rose.
'Call a doctor, hire a nurse!'
howled Uncle. 'Quick! It's getting worse.'
Auntie, with an evil grin,
attacked, and popped it with a pin.

Marian Swinger

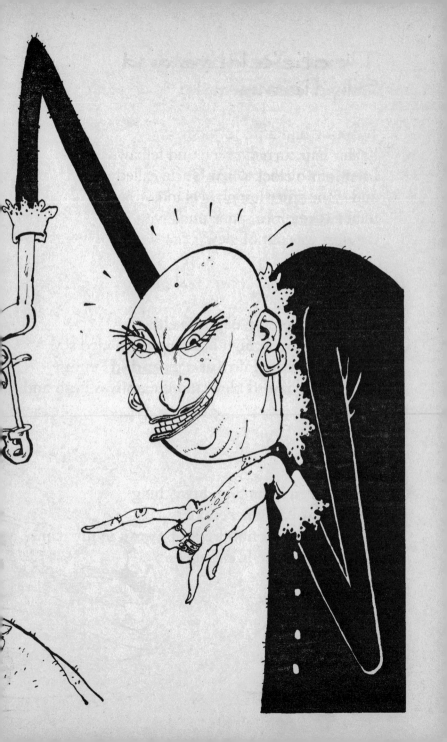

# Three Relatively Silly Poems

1.

I flew in a rocket to **ma's**
and some **mother** planets too,
then **father** into space until
the **son** was out of view.

2.

I remem-**brother** nights like this
with a full moon high in an **uncle**-ouded sky.
We were young. Life was a **grandad** venture.
A **niece twin**ned blew and the air was fresh and
    dry.

3.

**Wife** I been itching and twitching
as if I **dad** bad chickenpox?
Because I've got hundreds of **aunts** in my pants
a **nephew** more in my socks.

Nick Toczek

# Flo's Toe

Auntie Flo
Has a magic toe
That SHINES OUT in the gloom!
If she wakes with fright
In the middle of the night,
Her toe LIGHTS UP THE ROOM!

Trevor Harvey

# Ken

My bone idle cousin called Ken
Thinks he's a speckledy hen

Layabout?

Three eggs a day

Craig King

# Auntie Betty Thinks She's Batgirl

Auntie Betty pulls her cloak on
And the mask – the one with ears.
Almost ready, check the lipstick.
Wait until the neighbours cheer.
Through the window. What a leap!
She lands right in the driver's seat.
Off she goes with style and grace
To make our world a better place.

Andrea Shavick

## Auntie Dotty

My Auntie Dotty thought it nice
To twirl about upon the ice.
I warned her, people of proportions
Such as hers should take precautions,
But poor Auntie was so fond
Of skating on the village pond,
That she took no heed of warning
And went skating every morning.

Now we mourn for Auntie Dot:
The ice was thin, but she was not.

Colin West

# Relation Ships

I've got some strange relations
     (well really quite a few)
     a really odd collection
     a really motley crew . . .
         I'd like to send them sailing
         I'd like to see them go
         to France
         and other places
     *dans un grand bateau.*

There's sweaty Joe to start with
a galley slave for him . . .
     along with Auntie Nora
     and moaning Uncle Jim.

A one man sub for Frankie
         (so he can smoke alone)
         a coracle for Taffie
and a raft for cousin Joan.

For Auntie Maud and all her cats
I'd have a wooden ark
a lightship just for Tommy
         (who doesn't like the dark)

We'll find a log, half hollowed,
            for awkward Uncle Bill
            a kipper ketch for Charlie
            and a bloater boat for Jill.

For lumpy Uncle Harry
            I'll build a landing barge
      another for my sister
      and two for Auntie Marge.

I'll have a Nelson flagship
            for swanky Auntie Jan
a ferry boat for Jerry
and a pedalo for Pam.

I'll launch a great flotilla
relationships galore
but I'll keep the great Titanic
for the man who lives next door.

Peter Dixon

# My Uncle Percy Once Removed

My Uncle Percy once removed
his bobble hat, scarf, overcoat,
woolly jumper, string vest,
flared trousers and purple Y-fronts
and ran onto the pitch at Wembley
during a Cup Final
and was at once removed
by six stewards and nine officers of the law.
Once they'd caught him.

Paul Cookson

# Hush Hush

Norman is
a
secret agent.
Only family
and
close friends
know this.
Those of you
who have read
this poem
please
destroy it
and
forget
you ever
saw
it.

John C. Desmond

# Harmony in
# the Home

My mum
Does the puzzle
In the *Telegraph*.
My dad
Prefers the one
In the *Sun*.
So you see
We live in harmony –
There's never a crossword
Between them.

Pam Gidney

# Cousin Nell

Cousin Nell
married a frogman
in the hope
that one day
he would turn into
a handsome prince.

Instead he turned into
a sewage pipe
near Gravesend
and was never seen again.

Roger McGough

# The End of
# the World

Uncle Bill
Foretold the future.
The future from him
wasn't hid.
One day he predicted
the world would end.
And for him
it did.

Roger Stevens

# Listen

Have I ever told you of my Uncle Jack's
Wonderful collection of earhole wax.
He's got samples from:
Engin-ears
Buccan-ears
Volunt-ears
Musket-ears
Shakesp-eares
And one with snow on, labelled 'Mountain–ears'.

John Coldwell

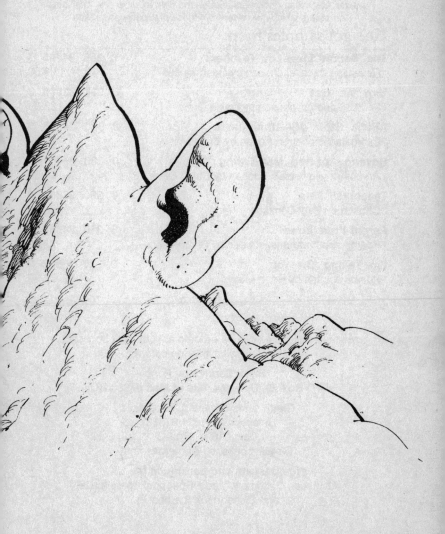

# A selected list of poetry books available from Macmillan

| | | | |
|---|---|---|---|
| **The Secret Lives of Teachers** | 0 | 330 | 34265 7 |
| Revealing rhymes, chosen by Brian Moses | | | £3.50 |
| **'Ere We Go!** | 0 | 330 | 32986 3 |
| Football poems, chosen by David Orme | | | £2.99 |
| **Aliens Stole My Underpants** | 0 | 330 | 34995 3 |
| Intergalactic poems chosen by Brian Moses | | | £2.99 |
| **Revenge of the Man-Eating Gerbils** | 0 | 330 | 35487 6 |
| And other vile verses, chosen by David Orme | | | £2.99 |
| **Teachers' Pets** | 0 | 330 | 36868 0 |
| Chosen by Paul Cookson | | | £2.99 |
| **Parent-Free Zone** | 0 | 330 | 34554 0 |
| Poems about parents, chosen by Brian Moses | | | £2.99 |
| **I'm Telling On You** | 0 | 330 | 36867 2 |
| Poems chosen by Brian Moses | | | £2.99 |